BURNIN' THOUGHTS

D. DAVIS

Copyright © 2018 D. Davis
Davis Publishing
All Rights Reserved.
ISBN-13: 978-0-692-16996-4

Design by Matthew Morse
Edited by Marley Harbuck Gibson

When my brain starts to wander

My thoughts begin to burn

And quickly I had to jot down

All the things I have learned

Over the years it was mostly from pain and love

But in the end burning thoughts is what it had turned.

If your brain doesn't battle with your heart,
the feelings may not be real.

BURNIN' THOUGHTS

Some people just don't want different; call that insane.

People ask for things they don't plan to commit to.

When you put 'em onto the things they're doing with their new boo. Just know, it's all cuz you made 'em feel something real.

I promised I'd wait while you found yourself,
but then I got tired of missing you.

I want [love] the things you don't see in yourself.

It's hard, but it's always necessary. [Growth]

Ladies, when life keeps throwing you bad guys, date lesbians. [LOL]

Adapt. Adjust. Experience [Life]

Explore. Discover. Conquer.
[The World]

I'm not interested in anything else
but you and this World.

Don't set permanent goals with temporary people.

If you don't plan to encourage or motivate your partner, at this point, you're an opponent.

These hoes talk a good game, but don't know how it's played.

My heart could recite a romance novel
and my mind could replay a nightmare.

Make sure your efforts are matched.
[Partnership]

I'm in love with her soul; that's why it's so hard to let go.

Once you get a real one, them other ones never make sense.

Tried to give her the World, but she settled for Georgia.

BURNIN' THOUGHTS

When they sleep on you,
make sure you wake 'em up to something new.

You were the only thing I've been sure about in my life, but I guess I wasn't so sure at all.
[LH]

If you have to choose me, then I'd never ask you to.

How do you expect me to change
when you want me to stay the same?

The power has always been YOU!

When I say, "She's beautiful," I'm not just talkin' 'bout her looks.
I'm speaking the language of the soul.

I've been a fool for love, but never a clown for you.

I've been torn, but never broken.

If you turned your back on me,
I hope you still marched forward.

Gotta learn to say "NO" sometimes and be selfish for your own sanity.

These people are in the game,
but they're playing EVERY position.
[Hoe]

When you love me,
I promise you'll understand [me] my heart.

These people want the trophy,
but they're tryin' ta play EVERY position.
[Focus]

I have scars only love can cover.
[Heal]

When you pluck that rare rose,
make sure you know how to water it.
[Nurture]

Don't give up until you're okay with the outcome or results.

Don't let your pride get in the way of your dignity.

We often speak of what we need,
yet end up only working for what we want.

Being in a box is what made something inside me go wild.

Man, she had me in my feelings.
She had me down bad.
I picked myself up and now all I can do is laugh.

BURNIN' THOUGHTS

I woke up today
and couldn't think of one thing
I could/should/would complain about.

I play good "D" and made her man man-up.

There's some dope ass shit out here in this World;
just make sure you see it.
[Travel]+[Fearless]

Don't ever count yourself out unless it's out to better things.

BURNIN' THOUGHTS

Defeat yesterday, EVERYDAY!!

Once a relationship is tarnished,
it's hard to clean and polish.

It's funny what you stumble upon
when you're not looking.

People underestimate the power of emotions.

You're either in the game or you're watching it.

Gotta look at shit for what it is
and not for what you wish and/or want it to be.

Anything lost can and will be found.

Never change up for the likes of any follower.
[Social Media]

Vibes so right anybody can feel me.

Don't let people's actions
or lack thereof change you.

I want what I want and I don't stop until I get just that.

We will find all we need when we stop looking.

What if the same thing that keeps you strong,
makes you weak?

You realize when you find yourself,
what you once thought was love, never was.

Communication is the key to wasted time.

Don't buy a Rolex for someone
who doesn't make time for you.

Traveling is the new black.

If you keep looking back,
you're going to trip moving forward.
If you keep stumbling backwards,
you'll never sprint ahead.

Your intuition is the Universe's way
of showing you the path.

Never disrespect a woman/man who changed your life.

She was a free spirit; she flowed with the wind.

Don't let anybody corrupt your energy.

Don't let anybody disrupt your soul.

Sometimes you simply need a confirmation
that you're appreciated.

Traveling is the new liquor
Culture is the new drug
Love is the new high
So pick your vice.

No matter how much time you invest,
you'll never get to go back.

Some things in life are harder to get through.
Life's a test. Doesn't mean give up.

I will change my entire World just to be in yours.

Ignoring calls I use to answer on the first ring.

Does distance make the heart grow closer or colder?
Fonder or Further?

Can't maintain a happy life
worrying about the actions of others.

Continue to be you;
The right person will never make you feel worthless.

I'm a sucka for a lot of things, just not you.

Once you hit the gas,
it's hard to slow down for people not going your speed.

Happiness looks gorgeous on you.

My brain is consumed with thoughts of you.

Build with a selfish woman and she'll tear it down with a new n*gga.

Ignoring notifications I use to run to the phone for.

You're worth more than late night phone calls and "R U up?" text messages.

Have you ever been turned on by life?
Well, make sure you make love to it.

When you can communicate effectively with someone, that's a connection not most can have.

The richest mindset will always learn to adapt and withstand time.

It takes time, so be patient with yourself.

Somewhere—right now—someone is yearning
for your heart and soul.

Spent many nights with some bad bitches,
but it's time to spend forever with a great woman.

Don't focus on changing your ways
(that's who you are);
focus on changing your mindset
(that's who you'll become).

Instead of meeting me in the middle,
let's find our way together.
Instead of meeting for a moment,
let's take this journey forever.

Be committed to being a better person.

Pay attention to your partner's needs
and that will satisfy their wants
before they ever crave anything.

Love your lows until you get high off of them.

Don't let it change you, let it guide you.

Just because we're not together
doesn't mean I stopped wanting the best for you.

Even if you don't know where you're going,
you know exactly who you want to go with.

Quit runnin' after the ones who love to be chased.
(They'll never slow down for you.)

The goal isn't to *fall* in love; it's to *stay* in love.

There's nothing better than a secret
only the two of us knows.

We're smart before we become dumb.
(Just let that sink in.)

Once you stop giving a fuck
about the opinions of others,
you'll live a life you never knew existed.

What if the same thing that brings you peace,
wreaks havoc?

I've craved many things,
but nothing can beat this addiction to love.

Make her smile daily; she'll always remember you.

Give your partner memorable experiences
and I promise they'll never forget you.

If I have to question your love, I don't need the answer.

The heart loves what the mind has learned to hate.

In this World of abandoned hearts, I'll find you.

I've been territorial over the wrong territory

My new love/partner/relationship is the World…
I'm going to give it love and explore
every beautiful inch of it.

Never claimed to be perfect
but to the right one; I'm definitely worth it.

Our most adventurous times
seem to be the ones unexpected.

Butterflies flying.
Flowers blooming.
People's smiles.

You notice the beauty in the World
when you live in a positive light.

Love at first VIBE.

If I didn't post it on the gram [Insta], it didn't happen.

I gave to you what I didn't have.

A man who can't is a man who won't.

I crave you more than any drug; for you I'm a fiend.

Make yourself uncomfortable sometimes
so you'll never be comfortable being uncomfortable.

Do things you never thought you'd do
with the people you've always wanted to do them with.

Oftentimes we don't learn the lesson until class is over.

Get away from those "let's go to the club" spirits and get around those "let's meet at the library" vibes.

You don't have to be perfect, just perfect to me.

Repeat after me: I can accomplish
and have all that I desire.

Trust is the glue that holds love together.

Loving and accepting your lowest flaws
will give you the highest form of security.

Even if I could build the perfect person,
I'd still choose you.

If you don't learn from your mistakes,
you'll never possess the wisdom to be wise.

Cheers to the long distances and the people in 'em.
(from a drunk night with J.Beaux & Nique)

Find what gives you purpose and live for it each day.

Many broken plates can lead to a full kitchen.

The truth is… I still forgive you.

When she crosses my mind, I taste my lips.

I'm ready to start the beginning of the "rest of my life."

I wish it wasn't too soon to tell you, "I love you."

You are ENOUGH.
[SELF]

I like you baby, good night.

Our energy and vibrations
will have our souls ringing as one.

I want to hear from you!

Follow @Burnin_Thoughts on Instagram and post your own Burnin' Thoughts with #BurninThoughts.

www.ingramcontent.com/pod-product-compliance
Lightning Source LLC
LaVergne TN
LVHW051607070426
835507LV00021B/2823